Mother Teresa

History Maker Bios

Jennifer A. Miller

BARNES & NOBLE

NEW YORK

To the One whom Mother Teresa served
and to my husband, both dear friends

Text © 2009 by Jennifer A. Miller
Illustrations © 2009 by Lerner Publishing Group, Inc.

This 2009 edition published by Barnes & Noble, Inc.
by arrangement with Lerner Publications Company, a division of
Lerner Publishing Group, Inc., Minneapolis, MN.

Illustrations by Tad Butler

ISBN-13: 978-1-4351-1405-0
Printed and bound in the United States of America

1 3 5 7 9 10 8 6 4 2

The quotes in this book have been drawn from many sources, and are assumed to be accurate as quoted
in their previously published forms. Although every effort has been made to verify the quotes and sources,
the publishers cannot guarantee their perfect accuracy.

All Web sites and URLs in this book are current at the point of publication. However, Web sites may be
taken down and URLs may change after publication without notice. The Publisher and the Author are
not responsible for the content contained in any specific Web site featured in this book, nor shall they be
liable for any loss or damage arising from the information contained in this book.

TABLE OF CONTENTS

INTRODUCTION

Mother Teresa grew up in Skopje, Macedonia, a country in southeastern Europe. Her parents taught her always to help the poor. The family had a strong faith in God. At eighteen, Mother Teresa decided to dedicate her life to God.

She taught school for seventeen years. Then she felt God call her to work with the poorest of the poor. She started her own religious community. Their work spread across the world. They helped the old, the orphaned, and the sick. They helped anyone in need.

World leaders began to notice and then to listen to Mother Teresa. She said the most important thing in life was to show love to every person. Her work and life touched people from many races, religions, and countries.

This is her story.

1 CHILDHOOD UPS AND DOWNS

On November 26, 1910, a celebration was taking place in Skopje, a busy city in Macedonia. A family welcomed their youngest child into the world. The baby girl was born to Nikola and Dranafile Bojaxhiu (bo-ya-JEE). A day later, the proud parents baptized her. They called her Agnes Gonxha (GOHN-jeh). *Gonxha* means "flower bud."

Agnes was the couple's fifth child. Two of their children had died, but two others had lived. Lazar, their son, was seven years old. Their older daughter, Aga, was three years old.

The Bojaxhiu house was near the center of the city. Their house was often full of people. Nikola and Dranafile (also called Drana) liked having people come to visit, especially the poor. They often gave money, food, and clothes to the poor. Drana said it was important to share food with anyone that was hungry.

The city of Skopje is very old. This five-hundred-year-old stone bridge crosses a river in the middle of Skopje.

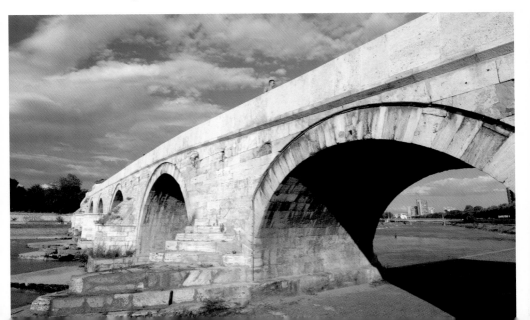

Nikola and Drana also liked to go to church. They went to a Roman Catholic church called the Sacred Heart Parish. They prayed together every night. Their faith led them to help anyone they could. To them, helping people was showing love.

People respected Agnes's parents. Nikola was a businessman and city council member (someone who helps make decisions about running a city). He spoke five languages. And he had many friends. Drana stayed home to take care of the children. She would do anything for them. But she said they had to set an example for others.

Agnes stands with her mother, Drana Bojaxhiu.

Twelve-year-old Agnes (LEFT) and Aga wear traditional Macedonian clothing.

The family lived a comfortable life. They even owned two houses. Nikola was a store owner. He traveled a lot for his business. The children always looked forward to his return. He would bring back many gifts. But most of all, the children loved to hear about his travels. They would gather around him to hear about his adventures.

Sometimes Nikola traveled with the other city council members. On the way back from one of these trips, he fell ill. Nikola died in 1918. Agnes was just eight years old.

This Bojaxhiu family portrait shows (FROM LEFT TO RIGHT) Lazar, Agnes, Drana, and Aga around 1927.

It was a sad time for the whole family. They did not have much money. Drana had to work to feed her children. She sewed and did embroidery. Drana wanted to provide a stable and happy life for her children. The family struggled to get by. But Drana still opened her home to anyone who was hungry.

Agnes liked school. She went to public school. But she also attended classes at her church. During church, young Agnes heard stories about missionaries. Missionaries travel to faraway countries to help people. They also teach others about their religion. Agnes loved to listen to stories about missionaries.

At the age of twelve, Agnes decided what she wanted to do when she grew up. She wanted to help the poor. She wanted to become a missionary. A few years later, missionaries came to speak at her church. They told stories about the poor people living in Bengal, India. Agnes decided she wanted to help those poor people.

Poor women and children wait in a food line in India.

When Agnes turned eighteen, she decided to become a missionary nun. A nun takes vows of poverty, purity, and obedience. She devotes her life to God. Agnes wanted to go to Loreto convent school in Dublin, Ireland. Besides training new nuns, the Loreto nuns also ran a girls school in Calcutta, India. Agnes hoped she would be sent there. In the fall of 1928, Agnes went to Dublin. Her childhood dreams were coming true. She would become a missionary in India.

THE BOJAXHIU FAMILY, SEPARATED

Lazar moved to Albania in 1925 when Agnes was just fourteen years old. After Agnes left to become a nun, Aga left Skopje to live with Lazar. Lazar and Aga convinced their mother to join them in Albania. But in 1939, Lazar moved away. Drana and Aga remained in Albania. Neither Lazar nor Agnes ever saw their mother and sister again. In 1972, Drana died in Albania. Two years later, Aga died.

2 SISTER TERESA, TEACHER

At the Dublin convent school, Agnes worked hard. She learned English as part of her training. In India, the nuns taught school in English. Later, she also learned the Bengali and Hindi languages that are spoken in India.

Agnes, now known as Sister Mary Teresa (TOP ROW ON THE RIGHT), stands with other nuns from Loreto.

Six weeks later, Agnes completed her training. This was the first step toward becoming a nun. She chose a new name, Sister Mary Teresa. The new name represented her new life. Agnes chose the name Teresa in honor of Saint Thérèse of Lisieux. She was the patron saint of missions. Saint Thérèse could do only small tasks. But she did them with great love.

Sister Mary Teresa left Ireland by boat for India. The trip was a long one. She arrived in Bombay, India. Next, she traveled overland to Calcutta. Finally, she rode a train to a Loreto convent in Darjeeling. Darjeeling is in the Himalayan Mountains. New nuns learned the basics of their religious life there. They also trained for their particular jobs. Sister Mary Teresa learned how to teach.

On May 23, 1929, Sister Mary Teresa finished her training. She became a Loreto novice, or a nun in training. Then she received her habit. A habit is the clothing that a nun wears.

Darjeeling is a mountain town in India. The area is famous for the tea that is grown there.

Sister Teresa smiles in a nun's plain dress and veil.

On May 24, 1931, she took her first vows as a nun. She promised to lead a life of poverty, purity, and obedience. She changed her name to Sister Teresa. She began to teach at Saint Mary's High School. Saint Mary's was a school for girls in Calcutta. Most of the girls were from middle- and upper-class families. But the nuns also taught orphan girls.

Sister Teresa loved teaching. She taught geography, history, and English. But the students' lessons didn't just happen in the classroom. Groups of girls went to the local hospital to help care for the sick. Other groups went into poor neighborhoods and slums to help the poor. Then they told Sister Teresa what they had seen and done.

On May 24, 1937, Sister Teresa took her final vows. She had finished her training. She promised to dedicate her life to God. She became Mother Teresa. And she continued to teach at the school in Calcutta.

A nun teaches children in a school for the poor in Calcutta.

Then World War II (1939–1945) began. Some teachers and students moved out of Calcutta. Convents in the country were safer than those in the city. But Mother Teresa stayed. She became the principal of the school. She also continued to teach. Her courage inspired the students and other nuns.

THE POOREST OF THE POOR

The Motijil slum was directly behind the Loreto convent. The people were very poor. Shacks were everywhere. People did not have enough to eat. They slept on the ground. Many suffered from diseases. Many lost hope that their lives could ever improve. World War II and a famine in 1943 resulted in more homelessness and poverty. Many poor people went to Calcutta to find work or food. During the war, mothers left their babies on the doorstep of the convent. They could no longer feed their children, but they knew the nuns would.

Mother Teresa loved teaching. But she felt the need to do more. She wanted to help the poor. They often had no one to take care of them. Sometimes they died alone.

In the fall of 1946, Mother Teresa had worked herself sick. Her superiors thought she might have tuberculosis, a serious lung disease. She went to Darjeeling to rest. During the train ride, Mother Teresa felt God was calling her again. He was telling her to serve the poor. She was to live among them. Mother Teresa returned to Calcutta. She told some of the other nuns about her calling. They had mixed reactions. But Mother Teresa had a new purpose for her life.

While riding a train on this Darjeeling train line, Mother Teresa felt called to serve the poor.

Mother Teresa told the archbishop about her calling. A high-ranking person within the Catholic Church, the archbishop was in charge of the area where Mother Teresa's convent and school were. Mother Teresa told him that she needed to leave the convent to help the poor. Mother Teresa was determined. Finally, the archbishop agreed. In February 1948, he sent the request to the pope in Rome. The pope is the leader of the Roman Catholic Church. Mother Teresa needed his permission. After some time, he agreed to her plan.

On November 16, 1948, Mother Teresa walked out of the Loreto convent into the darkness of night. She left the work, the students, and the nuns she so dearly loved. She entered the streets of Calcutta. Mother Teresa was alone. She was about to begin a new life among the poor.

3 DETERMINED TO WORK

Mother Teresa traveled by train to the Holy Family Hospital in Patna, about 290 miles away. There, she received medical training. She learned about various diseases and sores and how to treat them.

She also visited the slums in Patna. She practiced treating sick people in a clinic in Patna too. She worked hard to learn all she could.

At the end of 1948, she returned to Calcutta. She dressed as Indian women dressed. She wore sandals and a sari. A sari is a large piece of cloth that many Indian women wear over their head or one shoulder. Her new superior, Archbishop Ferdinand Périer, helped find a place for her to stay. She lived with the Little Sisters of the Poor, another group of nuns. They ran a home for the elderly poor.

Mother Teresa wears her blue and white sari while visiting a mission house.

Mother Teresa visits with poor children and their parents at a school in Calcutta.

In the beginning, Mother Teresa taught only five children under a tree. She wrote the Bengali alphabet in the dirt. She taught the children of the poor how to care for themselves. Soon her little class had grown to thirty students. The adults saw what she was doing for their children. Then they let her visit them in their homes.

The people of Calcutta admired what Mother Teresa was doing. Donations began to come in. She received a chalkboard, chalk, and chairs.

Soon, Mother Teresa moved into the second floor of a family's house. It was much closer to the slum. The next month, Mother Teresa's first volunteer arrived. She took Mother Teresa's birth name, Agnes. Sister Agnes was a former student of Mother Teresa. They became close friends.

One year after Mother Teresa moved into the house, five more volunteers joined her. As their numbers grew, the women took over the second floor. Eventually, they also used another part of the house.

14 CREEK LANE

The Little Sisters of the Poor's home for the elderly was one hour's walk from the slums. Father Celeste Van Exem helped Mother Teresa find lodging that was closer. He asked Michael Gomes about his large house at 14 Creek Lane. Gomes let Mother Teresa stay for free on the second floor. When Sister Agnes came to help, Gomes also let them use the top floor.

Mother Teresa speaks to a family from Calcutta. A group of her volunteers waits nearby.

The lifestyle of Mother Teresa and the volunteers was simple. They ate precooked wheat, rice, vegetables, a thin wheat soup, and vitamins. They each had one plate, one fork, one knife, and one spoon. They washed with the same bar of soap that they used to wash their clothes. They each had one straw mattress and one set of sheets. They had three sets of clothes. Two were for everyday wear. The other one was for special occasions.

Mother Teresa comforts a sick, homeless boy from a Calcutta slum.

Mother Teresa and the volunteers worked in five different slums. They treated the sick with medicines. They nursed people who were dying of hunger and tuberculosis. They cleaned and bandaged wounds. If anyone wanted to go to Mass (a Catholic church service) on Sunday, the group of women took them. People were always happy to see Mother Teresa and the volunteers.

The volunteers woke before sunrise. They prayed and went to Mass at Saint Teresa's Church. After eating breakfast, they visited each slum. Then they went home for lunch, housework, and a rest. They prayed and had afternoon tea. Then they returned to the city. Later, they went home for dinner, prayers, and mending. Then the volunteers had free time. Before going to bed, they prayed.

But Mother Teresa didn't go to bed. She wrote letters to people and rules for her followers. These rules were called the constitutions. They explained how the new group of nuns, called a religious order, would work and live. She sent the constitutions to the pope for approval.

In October 1950, Mother Teresa received approval to start a new order of nuns. It was called the Missionaries of Charity.

4 A NEW SOCIETY OF NUNS

Mother Teresa and her eleven novices continued to work with the poorest of the poor. As time went by, more and more women came to Mother Teresa. They wanted to join in her work. She soon realized she would need a larger home for her novices.

Finally, they bought a large house. Many more workers could fit into this new home. They had more space, but times were tough. Often it seemed that they wouldn't even have food to eat. But then food donations would arrive at just the right time. They never begged for their own needs. They begged only for the needs of the poor.

On April 12, 1953, the original eleven volunteers took their first vows as Missionaries of Charity. Mother Teresa took her final vows as a Missionary of Charity. She then became its mother superior and director.

Mother Teresa gives rice to poor women. The Missionaries of Charity gave away most of the food they collected.

Local leaders were happy to see the poor getting help. City officials let the nuns use a building next to a Hindu temple. (Hinduism is the main religion in India.) This became Mother Teresa's first home for the dying. Some Hindu people didn't like it that Christian nuns were so close to their temple. But the Hindus quickly realized that the nuns were doing good things.

Mother Teresa's first home for the dying (BELOW) was called Nirmal Hriday. The name means "pure heart."

Volunteers feed children at Mother Teresa's home for orphans.

Just two and a half years later, Mother Teresa opened her first children's home. The nuns cared for sick, crippled, or unwanted babies and children. Many were starving. Others had tuberculosis. Mother Teresa's goal was to cure these children. Then, if they had parents, they could go back to live with them.

Some children had parents that couldn't take care of them. Others were orphans. Mother Teresa helped both groups get an education or training. Then, when they became adults, they could get a job and provide for themselves. Many people gave money to help educate these children.

People adopted some of these children. Mother Teresa matched the child's religion to the adoptive parents' religion. Some children stayed with the nuns. But soon, Mother Teresa found another group of people who needed help—the lepers. These people had a disease called leprosy.

Leprosy affects the skin, nose, throat, eyes, and nervous system. If leprosy is not treated, people can lose the use of their hands and feet. But even more difficult than the sickness was people's fear of leprosy and of lepers. Lepers lost their jobs and many times their families. People were afraid they would get the disease if they touched a leper.

This Indian girl has leprosy on her hands and back. Her family depends on the Missionaries of Charity for food and medicine.

Leprosy can be treated with the right medicines. Mother Teresa started a leprosy clinic. She used a donated van. The van went to the lepers in the streets. The nuns treated the lepers with the latest medicines. In 1959, Mother Teresa and her nuns opened a leprosy hospital. Lepers who were very sick could be treated there. But Mother Teresa had an even bigger dream for lepers.

Poor people line up beside the Missionaries of Charity van to receive food and other supplies.

A volunteer watches herded geese at Mother Teresa's leper colony, Shanti Nagar.

Mother Teresa decided to open a leper colony. The Indian government gave the Missionaries of Charity thirty-four acres of land. Lepers lived and worked at the colony. They built their own homes. They grew crops, ran their own grocery store, and made baskets. They were able to take care of themselves.

Meanwhile, the needs in other parts of India were great as well. Before long, the Missionaries of Charity were running schools, homeless shelters, and nursery schools. They also provided aid for victims of natural disasters.

In 1963, Mother Teresa founded the Missionaries of Charity Brothers. In 1965, another country asked for help from Mother Teresa.

MOTHER TERESA, THE SPOKESWOMAN

The film *Something Beautiful for God* drew lots of media attention to Mother Teresa's work with the poor. At first, she was nervous about all the news coverage. But eventually, she realized she could use the attention to tell people about helping the poor. She could encourage people to care for the poor around them. In time, she began to speak more and more. She even learned to speak to groups from around the world. Her simple message touched millions.

5 GROWTH AND PRAISE

Bishop Benitez Barquisimeto asked Mother Teresa to open a home in Venezuela, a country in South America. Soon many other countries wanted Mother Teresa and her nuns to come. Italy, Tanzania, Australia, Jordan, Great Britain, and the United States all invited her to open missions for their needy people.

The nuns took care of the homeless, the poor, drug addicts, alcoholics, prisoners, AIDS patients, and juvenile delinquents. They also cared for the needy in war-torn nations.

The Missionaries of Charity were happy with their work. But they had sad times as well. Belfast, Ireland, was a city where two religious groups, Protestants and Catholics, fought each other. The city invited the nuns to set up a mission there. They did so. But soon, the sisters were made to feel unwanted, so they left. In Kilburn, London, someone set fire to a Missionaries of Charity mission house. Twenty-one people died. They never found the person who set the fire.

Prince Charles of Great Britain visited Mother Teresa on a trip to Calcutta.

Still, many people of all faiths respected Mother Teresa's work. They considered her a holy person. In 1969, reporter Malcolm Muggeridge made a film about the work of the missionaries. He called it *Something Beautiful for God*. He then wrote a book by the same name. The world began to take notice of the nun's passion and commitment.

CRITICISM OF MOTHER TERESA

Mother Teresa became a world figure. With this fame came criticism. A journalist named Christopher Hitchens wrote a book about Mother Teresa. He said she accepted $1.5 million from Charles Keating. He was a man who had cheated others out of money. He served ten years in prison. But Mother Teresa did not apologize. And she refused to give the money back. She felt the money was God's gift to the poor.

Mother Teresa received an honorary degree in medicine from the Catholic University of the Sacred Heart in Rome.

Soon several nations, including India, Italy, Great Britain, the United States, and the country then known as the Soviet Union, gave Mother Teresa awards. By 1979, Mother Teresa had set up 158 missions throughout the world. All kinds of people—priests, monks, children, married people, and people from different religions—helped do the work that Mother Teresa had started. In addition, Mother Teresa created a new branch called the Contemplative Brothers, who dedicated themselves to the study of the scriptures.

*Mother Teresa
receives the Nobel
Peace Prize from
the chairman
of the Nobel
Committee.*

That same year, Mother Teresa won the
Nobel Peace Prize. The prize is awarded to
a person from anywhere in the world who
has done important work for peace and
understanding.

Mother Teresa didn't prepare her speech
ahead of time. Instead, she prayed. Her
message of loving God through helping
others moved the people at the ceremony.
A Norwegian journalist wrote, "How good
it is to [see the] press . . . spellbound by a
real star, with a real glitter. . . . [Mother
Teresa's] only thought is how to use the
Nobel Prize in the best possible way for the
world's poorest of the poor."

Mother Teresa's simple message of love even influenced world leaders. President Ronald Reagan listened to Mother Teresa when she visited him in 1981. Within a few months, she visited Northern Ireland. Protestants and Catholics were fighting about control of their country. Mother Teresa talked about peace between the two groups. Even in war-torn Beirut, Lebanon, she convinced troops to stop shooting. She then helped thirty-seven children escape the dangerous area.

Mother Teresa greets a boy orphaned by war in Beirut.

Children surround Mother Teresa during a ceremony at her orphanage in Calcutta in 1980.

Nothing, it seemed, would slow her down. But finally, her health did. Mother Teresa had a heart attack in 1983. Five years later, doctors gave her a pacemaker. This device helped her heart function correctly.

She also came down with malaria in 1993 at the age of eighty-two. Malaria is a serious disease spread by mosquitoes. In 1996, she was hospitalized for a malaria attack. While in the hospital, she suffered two more heart attacks. She also developed an illness called pneumonia.

Finally, in January 1997, Mother Teresa stepped down as head of her order. By March, the Missionaries of Charity chose Sister Nirmala to replace Mother Teresa. Sister Nirmala had been born a Hindu. She became a Catholic and joined the Missionaries of Charity.

On September 6, 1997, Mother Teresa ate dinner, said her prayers, and went to bed. A little while later, her heart finally stopped. But she had lived up to her name. Like Saint Thérèse of Lisieux, she had done small things with great love. And, in the end, Mother Teresa had also done great things with great love.

Sister Nirmala (LEFT) listens as Mother Teresa speaks to news reporters about helping the poor.

TIMELINE

In the year . . .

1928 Agnes left home to begin training as a nun.

1931 she took her first vows as a nun, changed her name to Sister Teresa, and began teaching at Saint Mary's High School in Calcutta, India.

1937 Sister Teresa took her final vows as a nun. she became Mother Teresa.   Age 27

1946 she felt God call her to work with slum dwellers.

1948 she began her work in the slums of Calcutta.   Age 38

1950 she began the Missionaries of Charity.

1953 she established her first home for the dying.

1955 she opened a home for children.

1957 she started her first mobile leprosy clinic.

1959 she opened a hospital for lepers.

1965 she opened a leprosy colony and her first house outside of India in Venezuela.

1979 she won the Nobel Peace Prize in Oslo, Norway.   Age 69

1983 she had a heart attack.

1993 she came down with malaria.

1997 she died on September 6.   Age 86

FUNERAL

Mother Teresa lay in an open casket with an Indian flag draped across it. Thousands of people lined up at Saint Thomas Church in Calcutta to see her one last time. She wore her typical blue-bordered white sari and held in her hands a cross and rosary. (This string of beads is used in the Catholic Church for counting prayers.)

The Indian government held a state funeral one week later at Netaji stadium. World leaders, the poor, and people from many faiths were present. Bible readings were delivered in Bengali and Hindi. Mother Teresa's coffin was carried to its final resting place. The coffin was laid in a tomb in one of the first houses the order owned. It is called the Mother House. About one million people lined the streets of Calcutta to see Mother Teresa's coffin pass by.

Thousands of people lined up to pay their last respects to Mother Teresa.

FURTHER READING

Demi. *Mother Teresa*. New York: Margaret K. McElderry, 2005. This picture-book biography pairs Mother Teresa's life story with beautiful artwork.

Dils, Tracey E. *Mother Teresa*. New York: Chelsea House Publications, 2001. This biography is accompanied by black-and-white photographs.

Morgan, Nina. *Mother Teresa: Saint of the Poor*. Orlando, FL: Steck-Vaughn, 1998. This photo essay describes Mother Teresa's life.

Mother Teresa. *Stories Told by Mother Teresa*. Dorset, UK: Element Books, 2000. This book presents a retelling of eleven of Mother Teresa's favorite stories, accompanied by full-spread illustrations.

Ransom, Candice F. *Mother Teresa*. Minneapolis: Millbrook Press, 2001. Full-page artwork complements this early-reader biography.

Rice, Tanya. *The Life and Times of Mother Teresa*. New York: Chelsea House Publications, 1998. The author deftly retells the life of Mother Teresa.

WEBSITES

Mother Teresa—Biography
http://nobelprize.org/nobel_prizes/peace/laureates/ 1979/teresa-bio.html The Nobel Foundation site presents the Mother Teresa's lecture at the Nobel Prize ceremony as well as a biography, documentary, and other resources.